IMAGES OF ENGLAND

BAKEWELL
AND THE WHITE PEAK

IMAGES OF ENGLAND

BAKEWELL
AND THE WHITE PEAK

PETER TUFFREY

TEMPUS

This book is dedicated to Geoff Thomas – thanks for your help once more.

Frontispiece: Stanton Ford, Calver, viewed from the River Derwent.

First published 2003

Tempus Publishing Limited
The Mill, Brimscombe Port,
Stroud, Gloucestershire, GL5 2QG

© Peter Tuffrey, 2003

British Library Cataloguing in Publication Data.
A catalogue record for this book is available from the British Library.

ISBN 0 7524 3042 4

Typesetting and origination by Tempus Publishing Limited
Printed in Great Britain by Midway Colour Print, Wiltshire

Contents

Above: At the Surprise near Hathersage.

Left: The impressive Runic Cross in All Saints churchyard at Bakewell. This is one of two ninth-century Saxon crosses in the churchyard. It is the larger of the two crosses and leans at a slight angle in a fenced enclosure near the south transept. The detail in the carving showing spiral vine-scroll motifs, animals and scenes from Christ's life is still reasonably well preserved. During the restoration of the church in the 1840s many fine carved fragments of Saxon stonework and some ancient coffins were found. Some of these can be seen in and around the church porch.

Introduction

In 1996 I compiled a book of Edgar Leonard Scrivens' pictures of Doncaster. Four years later I produced another book: *In and around Rotherham from the Scrivens' Collection*. Now in 2003, I am pleased to offer a third book of the noted photographer's pictures – *Bakewell and the White Peak*.

In the autumn of 1985, I journeyed south to meet Scrivens' only surviving daughter, Ivy. From her I learned that Edgar was born in 1883 and first became interested in photography when he was at school, obtaining his first camera whilst still a pupil. Initially he worked as a press photographer, establishing a photographic business in Cooper Street, Hyde Park, Doncaster during the first decade of the twentieth century. Amongst the other photographic companies in Doncaster at this time were Don Lion, Arjay Productions, Empire Views, Regina Company Press and J. Simmonton & Son. All the people involved with these companies produced picture postcards, but Scrivens was to become the leading exponent of this trade, not only in his home town but arguably throughout South Yorkshire, North Derbyshire and Nottinghamshire too. This was because during the ensuing thirty years he captured in his postcards almost every main road, street or thoroughfare in nearly every town and village within a forty-mile radius of Doncaster. He also took pictures in Whitby, York and London.

Each Scrivens' postcard bears his unmistakeable initials E.L.S., and he evolved a meticulous numbering system for his cards. On one numbered 191-24, the first number denotes the locality, in this case 191 relates to Bakewell. The second number indicates that the postcard is the 24th in the Bakewell series. Scrivens photographed over 250 localities, with a fair number of cards in each series.

Over the years, Scrivens' postcards have grown in popularity, which is reflected in the prices paid for them by postcard dealers and collectors. His pictures show scenes prior to industrial, commercial or road developments and this is what makes his pictures so fascinating. Yet he was not frightened about being bold and photographing whatever interested him, and chancing his arm over the subject's commercial viability.

This is shown in the pictures reproduced in this book of the Toad Mouth Rock at Hathersage, Millers Dale and the countless church interiors which seemed to fascinate him so much. Yet some of his pictures can be so breathtaking such as Calver from Curbar, Mam Tor at Castleton and Froggatt Edge from Stoke Hall.

Scrivens' postcard views have outstanding clarity, are beautifully composed and full of incidental detail. An example of the latter may be seen in a street scene at Castleton, where an old man and young girl pose in the street. Scrivens seemed to have the knack of persuading anyone to pose in his views, adding charm and interest to the scene. During the 1920s and 1930s, Scrivens re-photographed a number of locations already recorded earlier in his career, adding the letter 'V' or 'G', depending on the period, to the numbering on the cards. It is believed that the 'V' and 'G' represent dates from the 1920s and the 1930s respectively; cards from Scrivens' earlier postcards were not marked in this way and are believed to be from the period between 1905-'20.

By the 1920s, Scrivens had moved his photographic business to Queen's Road, Wheatley, Doncaster, whilst living with his wife and two daughters in Craithie Road, Doncaster. At this time his postcard and developing/printing business flourished. His postcard views could be found in a variety of outlets including newsagents and stationers. Scrivens' daughter Ivy remembers that the Queen's Road premises were methodically organized to accommodate the various photographic processes, with up to twenty-five people being employed to cope with the workload. She also recalls that her father rarely brooded on matters and often arrived home in the evenings whistling *Tip-toe Through the Tulips*. He had virtually no other interests apart from photography, and frequently lectured on the subject to local camera clubs and other photographic societies.

When Scrivens died in 1950 and his business was sold, no one bothered to save the thousands of postcard-view negatives neatly filed in pigeon holes in an upstairs room at Queen's Road. Nobody appreciated their worth or could ever have envisaged that Scrivens would become one of the region's major topographical artists. At one time, there was a strong local rumour that a subsequent owner of the Queen's Road premises dumped the glass-plate negatives in a hole on the site and covered them with concrete. However, having contacted the person who was said to have done this, the allegation was strenuously denied!

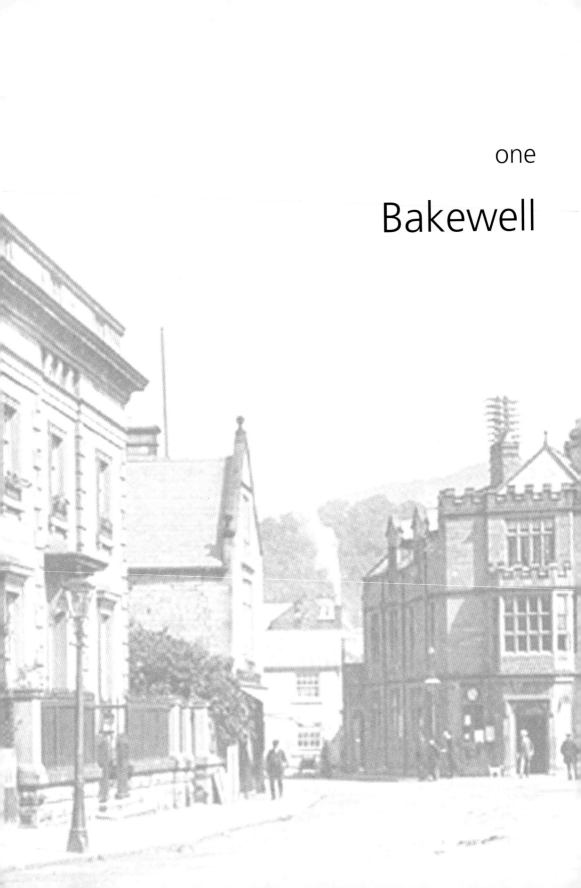

one

Bakewell

Rutland Square, Bakewell, created in 1804, with the Red Lion Hotel on the right. The Duke of Rutland attempted to re-model Bakewell around 1800. He wanted the area to be a spa town to rival the one owned by the Duke of Devonshire at Buxton. In making these alterations the Duke of Rutland altered a number of streets and built stone houses to replace ones incorporating timber frames. The ancient core of Bakewell was designated a Conservation Area in 1980, thus ensuring the character of the town could be maintained.

A similar view of Rutland Square to the one above. Bakewell, dating from Saxon times, and situated on the Wye, is a popular tourist area and is at the heart of the Peak District National Park. It was formerly connected with the Vernon family and, in time, the Manners family. In the Domesday Book Bakewell appears as *Badequella* meaning Badecca's Well or Bath-well.

Bakewell with All Saints Church to the right. The materials used in building many Bakewell properties were local stone and grit stone, the latter being coarse sandstone. Bakewell is well known for the famous Bakewell pudding. The area also has one of the oldest markets, dating from at least 1300. The first noted fair was staged there in 1254.

The pointed-arched bridge and weir at Bakewell. The town's position on the crossing point of the river is a reason given for its early growth. This was helped in later years by utilising water power from the Wye.

Paxton and his assistant John Robertson designed Burton Close, situated off Haddon. It was built between 1845-'48 for Quaker banker and stockbroker, John Allcard, and his unmarried daughter. The interior included a two-storey Great Hall and an impressive staircase, yet there were only two principal bedrooms. Pugin was responsible for much of the internal fitting up and decoration. Pevsner in *Derbyshire* (1953) describes Burton Close as 'a virtual epitome of Early Victorian taste.' T.D. Barry of Liverpool transformed it into a mansion during the latter half of the nineteenth century for William Allcard, surviving intact until 1949 when 'some demolition was begun, and the interior partially stripped'.

Bakewell viewed from Castle Hill, with All Saints Church on the left. The mound of Castle Hill is the site of a Norman castle. In AD 924 it is known that Edward the Elder (son of Alfred the Great) started work on a fort at Bakewell. An excavation in 1969 revealed that during the twelfth century a motte had been built to fortify a rubble rampart, square in plan and dating from an earlier period.

Church Street featuring the business premises of auctioneers, Marchant Brooks & Co. on the right; Barret, ladies and gents outfitters further along the street and All Saints Church on the hill in the centre. The church affords a panoramic view over the River Wye Valley. Much of Bakewell's early prosperity came from the wool trade and the lead mining industry.

The Holme footbridge and ford. This former packhorse bridge near Holme Hall dates from 1664. Its architectural features include five segmental arches, two smaller arches, cut waters and recesses.

Bakewell from the bridge, which dates from around 1300. It has five ribbed pointed arches with breakwaters.

Bath gardens with the Rutland Hotel on the right. The stone building, which replaced an earlier hotel, the White Horse Inn, comprises five bays and features a Tuscan Doric porch which is just discernable in the picture.

Above and below: In 1636 Lady Grace Manners devised a £15 yearly charge on land at Elton, for the provision of a school which was carried on under the terms of her will until 1874. The income was allowed to accumulate, until in 1893 it amounted to £1,250 and a scheme was propounded for the building of a new school. The County Council made an addition of £600 to the fund, and the school was re-opened in 1896 as a secondary school fully recognised by the Board of Education and aided by grants from the County Council. A new school, built at a cost of over £30,000, was opened in 1938. The picture above shows Lady Manners School, part of which is in a neo-Georgian style, in Shutts Lane. Castle Hill House (Lady Manners School Boarding House) dates from the late eighteenth century. Situated in Baslow Road it was formerly the residence of the Duke of Rutland's agent.

The Pack Horse Bridge, Bakewell, not far from Hall Holme Bridge, dates from 1664. It features five segmental arches, with two smaller arches cutwaters and recesses. Bakewell is seated at the foot of a hill on the western bank of the River Wye which rises near the Axe Edge Hill, Buxton, and divides this parish from Chapel-en-le-Frith, Hope and Tideswell, until it enters Monsal Dale, through which it flows, and then past the town of Bakewell into the Derwent, its whole course being about twenty-one miles. Extensive improvements in the Wye were undertaken by the direction of the eighth Duke of Devonshire, with a view to preventing the recurrence of 'disastrous inundations', and in 1884 the river was cleaned out between Bakewell and Ashford and an island subsequently named 'Tory Island' formed.

The Bridge, Bakewell, with All Saints Church in the distance.

Above: At the south end of All Saints Church is the monument of Dorothy Vernon and her husband, Sir John Manners, whose romantic marriage brought Haddon to the Manners family. The kneeling figures of John and his lady face each other beneath an arch in the centre. Between them is a pedestal with an inscription recording the death of the knight in 1611 and of his wife in 1584. Above is a shield with sixteen quarterings. On the cornice are other shields, and below the central figures are those of their four children.

Left: The Font in Bakewell Church is a large octagon bearing full-length figures under canopies, crudely carved on each of the eight faces, which may be assigned to the close of the thirteenth century.

Left: Holme Hall, Bakewell, dates from 1626 and was built by Bernard Wells. Amongst its architectural features are embattled, canted, side bay-windows.

Left below: On the Wye in Haddon meadows, Bakewell. At one time the Duke of Rutland was the lord of the manor, and R.W. Cockerton and Duncan Orme were the principal landowners in the area.

Below: The River Wye and Golf Links, Bakewell.

The Town Hall, at one time the property of the Bakewell Town Hall Company Limited, opened on 18 September 1890. It was built of stone in the Gothic style, from designs by George E. Statham, architect of Nottingham, and in plan takes the form of the letter 'L', giving a frontage to The Square and to Bath Street. At one time the Hall comprised an assembly room 64ft long and 34ft wide on the first floor, with a good stage for theatrical representations, and a spacious upper hall or landing, communicating with the stage, retiring and cloak rooms. There were also two large rooms, one of which was used by the Freemasons as a Lodge room, and the other for meetings of the Urban Council and town committees. The building also features a spacious stone staircase leading from the main entrance hall, which has a marble mosaic pavement, and is entered from The Square. On the ground floor was a courtroom used both by the magistrates and county court, and was also available for lectures, classes and smaller social gatherings.

The former Union Workhouse (later Newholme Hospital), in the Jacobean style, dates from 1841.

All Saints Church, standing on an eminence above the principal part of the town, is a large cruciform embattled structure, about 150ft in length and 105ft in breadth, including the transepts, and consists of chancel, clerestoried nave, aisles, porch, transepts and a central tower, rising from a square lower stage into a battlement octagon, with an elegant spire. The fabric exhibits remains of Norman work, including at the west end, a fine Norman doorway, with an arcading above it, and other portions belonging to a very early church, the first alterations being made in 1250, when the Early English style was well advanced. The chancel was rebuilt and considerably lengthened towards the commencement of the Decorated period, about 1300 or earlier, and the Vernon chapel, forming an eastern aisle to the south transept, was built about 1360. The octagonal tower and spire were erected on the Early English base at the end of the fourteenth or beginning of the fifteenth century, when also the clerestory was added, the roofs lowered and the whole of the parapets embattled. In 1825/26 the spire was removed, and in 1830 the tower also, owing to the unsafe condition of the piers. In 1841 extensive repairs of the whole fabric were begun, and completed in 1852, at a cost of £8,600. The register dates from 1614.

Panoramic view of Bakewell.

two

Baslow

Left, above: The River Derwent at Baslow.

Left: Street scene at Baslow. The lychgate and entrance to St Anne's Church may be seen to the right.

Below: The Eaglestone at Baslow.

Baslow with the Wheatsheaf Hotel on the right.

St Anne's Church, Baslow, is an ancient structure in the later English style, with nave, chancel side aisles and tower, a low spire at the western end of the north aisle and six bells. In 1853 it was completely restored, new seated and the chancel rebuilt a cost of about £1,200 by the Duke of Devonshire. Those involved with the work included Paxton and his son-in-law G.H. Stokes. The clock face in the tower of St Anne's Church commemorates Queen Victoria's Diamond Jubilee in 1897, with the twelve hours represented by the characters – V I C T O R I A 1 8 9 7 – the 'V' beginning at 9 o'clock. Edward Mason Wrench, who was the village doctor, designed the clock face.

Interior view of St Anne's Church, where the chancel was rebuilt in 1911.

The church door at Baslow.

The lectern and pulpit at Baslow Church.

Derwent View, Baslow. In *The National Gazetteer* (1868) it was stated: 'The village of Baslow, which is of considerable size, is pleasantly seated on the banks of the river Derwent, over which is an ancient stone bridge of three arches. It is about 1½ miles to the north of Chatsworth, and on the NE and W are a range of lofty hills, with extensive moors abounding in grouse. Many of the inhabitants are employed in the mills of the Calver Cotton-Spinning Company, which are situated a little lower down the river, at the village of Calver, where there is another bridge across the Derwent of modern construction. There is a National school, established in 1839 by the Duke of Rutland, who is lord of the manor. Baslow belongs to the honour of Tutbury, in the Duchy of Lancaster.'

The entrance to Chatsworth at Baslow.

Left, above: The Hydro, Baslow.

Left: Robin Hood Farm, near Baslow.

Below: Nether End, Baslow.

three

Calver

Calver street scene. In the *Directory of Sheffield and Twenty Miles Round* (1862) it is mentioned: 'Calver is a township and considerable but scattered village, on the bank of the river Derwent, and 4 ½ miles NNE from Bakewell, contains 710 acres, 1 rood, 15 perches of land, and in 1861 had 617 inhabitants. Col. Leslie is lord of the manor and principal owner. The township is noted for its lime, and here is an extensive cotton mill, near which gas works were erected in 1846. The mills, with several adjoining houses, are called Calver Bridge, where there is a school principally supported by the Calver Mill Co. It was licensed for divine service in 1850. Calver Sough is a district at the cross of the Chesterfield and Chapel-en-le-Frith, and Sheffield and Bakewell roads. The Bull's Head Inn, at Calver, affords every accommodation for visitors. It is neatly fitted up, and has been recently enlarged, when new stabling and lock-up coach houses were added. About the latter end of September, a large Annual Show is held here, for fruit, vegetables, flowers, etc. Mr Charles Slowe is the proprietor. Feast, first Sunday in August'.

Calver Bridge and Curbar, from St Mary's Woods, *c.* 1920.

View of Calver Bridge, *c.* 1925.

Looking along Cliffe Lane, Calver.

Above and below: Calver Mill, a six-storey structure, was built by Arkwright in 1803/4 to replace one dating from the late eighteenth century, around 1785. It was a thriving mill and employed many local hands. Cotton production ceased in 1923 but the building had a new lease of life as Colditz in the television series of the same name. The building presently comprises a number of flats.

A breathtaking view of Calver from Curbar. Earliest forms of industry in the village included lead mining and lime burning. Scrivens was obviously fascinated by the mill, as it appears in a number of his Calver views.

Calver from St Mary's Woods. During an exploration in 1860 remains of an early Anglo-Saxon settlement were revealed with skeletons found in a limestone rock.

Left: On the Derwent at Calver.

Below: New Bridge, Calver.

The post office, Calver.

Calver with photographer Edgar Leonard Scrivens' car in the foreground. Calver's population in the early 1930s, near the time the picture was taken, was 402.

Stocking Farm and Mill, Calver, from Curbar. Calver was formerly associated with cotton spinning and a fine seven-storey mill, which functioned as such between 1785-1920. It is still extant today and is found on the Derwent to the east of the main village at Calver Bridge just off the A623. It has since been converted into luxury apartments. The Bridge Inn is adjacent.

Stocking Farm, Calver.

Panorama of Calver. Calver village is centred around the Derwent Water Arms, a hundred metres off the other side of the main road, and has many attractive old houses.

Cliffe College, Calver, was an institution maintained by the Methodist Church for the training of lay preachers, and was the headquarters of the Gospel Car Mission, which employed a number of evangelists to visit the rural parts of England.

Left: Cook Memorial Wing, Cliffe College, Calver. In 1907 the college was enlarged by the erection of the Thomas Champness Memorial Wing, and in 1913 a wing was added in memory of the Revd Thomas Cook, first principal of the college.

Below: Cliffe College, Calver. In 1924 the Rt Hon. David Lloyd George OM, MP, opened another wing. In 1933 a memorial chapel was added to the Revd Samuel Chadwick. At one time the college owned a lot of land in the area. Cliffe College is now a Methodist training centre and a conference centre.

Above: Looking along Cliffe Lane, Calver.

Below: The Coronation Lamp at Calver.

Stanton Ford, Calver from the River Derwent.

Two views of the Derwentwater Arms public house. Amongst the other pubs in the area are the Eyre Arms and the nearby Bridge Inn (but this is really in Curbar).

Stoke Hall, Calver, a stately stone mansion, was built in 1757 for the Revd John Simpson. Speculation suggests that James Paine was responsible for some of the designs. The Hall comprises five by five bays, two-and-a-half storeys and has a west doorway with Tuscan columns. In *Old Halls, Manors and Families of Derbyshire, Volume I, The High Peak Hundred*, by Joseph Tilley, (transcribed by Rosemary Lockie), 1999-2000, it interesting to note: 'Few residences in the country are more delightfully situated than Stoke Hall. At the beginning of the present century the hall was held by one of the Arkwrights; its present owner is Alderman M. Hunter, JP, of the firm of Michael Hunter & Sons, of the Talbot Works, Savile Street, Sheffield, who makes it his summer residence. We are told that the hall is scarcely two centuries old, and that the architect was the one who designed the stables at Chatsworth. Writers, who visited the edifice more than a hundred years ago, speak of it then as old, but such conflicting assertions only point the finger of reproach at any of us who are Derbyshire men, for not showing more interest in the preservation of facts. We believe that the present structure was built during the tenure of the Cavendishes or Sacheverells; and in either case the assumption of White and Rhodes would be correct.'

The Old Toll Bar,
Calver.

The Vicarage, Calver.

Village scene at Calver.

Right, above: Calver village, *c.* 1912.

Right: Calver village, *c.* 1920.

Below: Calver with the church in the foreground.

Village scene, Calver, *c.* 1912.

Village scene, Calver, *c.* 1930.

four

Ashford,
Haddon Hall
and Sheldon

Above: Ashford-in-the-Water Holy Trinity Church underwent extensive rebuilding between 1868-'70 at the hands of J.M. & H. Taylor. A memorial to Henry Watson, who established a Marble Works in Ashford in 1748, may be seen in the church near the main door. Many members of the Cavendish family have lived in Ashford – at Churchdale Hall – and several of them are commemorated in the church where an old hatchment, dated 1724, is preserved, showing the Cavendish arms. William Cavendish, who married United States President John F. Kennedy's sister, Kathleen Agnes Kennedy, was born and raised in Churchdale Hall. He unfortunately died after five weeks of their marriage. Holy Trinity is one of only a few churches known to retain Maidens' funeral garlands. They were carried before the coffin at the funeral service of young girls who were unfortunate enough to die as maidens, and by a girl of a similar age to the deceased.

Above and below: Ashford was once well known for being at the heart of the black marble industry, Henry Watson's works, as already mentioned, being founded in 1748. The material was used in the manufacture of finely inlaid ornamental work. It was quarried from Kirk Dale and Rookery Wood just a short distance from Ashford. Watson also invented machinery for cutting and polishing the marble, which enabled it to be mass-produced and it became very popular. Ashford also displays a number of impressive eighteenth and nineteenth-century properties, some of which may be seen in these two views of Greaves Lane.

Oppposite below: Over the years Ashford, often described as a 'sleepy village', has become well known for its well-dressing festival, held every year around Ascension Day. Travelling north west, Ashford is further along the River Wye from Bakewell and boasts several ancient bridges, including Sheepwash and Mill Bridge. Dating from the seventeenth century, Sheepwash Bridge has a pen adjacent for 'sheepwashing' and this practice continued until recent times. Mill Bridge dates from the mid-1660s.

A water mill at Ashford, dating from around the eighteenth century. In the Domesday Book Ashford appears as *Aisseford*, a Saxon word meaning 'the ford of the ash'. The suffix '-in-the-Water' was recently adopted to distinguish this from the many other Ashfords in England.

The pump at Ashford.

Haddon Hall, a fine example of Britain's medieval manor houses, is one of the Duke of Rutland's seats, situated south of Bakewell, lying alongside the River Wye. Perhaps no other medieval house has withstood the passage of time so well. Because the Rutlands used the Hall very little during the eighteenth and nineteenth centuries, it has remained almost unaltered since the end of the sixteenth century. William the Conqueror's illegitimate son, Peveril, and his descendants held Haddon for a hundred years before it passed into the hands of the Vernons. The following four centuries saw the transformation from its Norman origins into the existing medieval and Tudor manor house. In the late sixteenth century, it passed through marriage to the Manners family, later to become the Dukes of Rutland, in whose hands it has remained.

During the 1920s the ninth Duke of Rutland came to realise the building's importance and undertook a sensitive restoration scheme. At one time Henry VIII's elder brother was a frequent guest at the Hall, but in recent times Haddon Hall has provided a popular location for film and television productions, including the feature films *Elizabeth* and *Jane Eyre*, and the television productions *The Prince and the Pauper* and *Moll Flanders*.

Left: Haddon Hall has some beautiful gardens. The terraced gardens, added during the sixteenth century, boast an array of roses, clematis and delphiniums. It is believed by many to be the most romantic garden in Britain.

Left below: View of Haddon Hall. The magnificent collection of English, Flemish and French tapestries is a special feature of Haddon Hall. But this is only a small proportion of the tapestries held by the house as many more were lost in a fire in 1925. It is thought that five of those surviving may have belonged to Charles I.

Below: Haddon Hall and stables, *c.* 1912.

Top: Haddon Hall from the River Wye, *c.* 1920.

Above: The ballroom (Long Gallery) at Haddon Hall is arguably one of Haddon's grandest rooms. It is a typical Elizabethan gallery and was built by John Manners in the late sixteenth and early seventeenth century. The furnishings are of varying dates and illumination is created by the unique use of diamond panes of glass in the windows. Access is gained to the Long Gallery by large oak steps, which are reputed to have been hewn from the roots of a single oak tree.

Left: The chapel is situated in the small parish of Nether Haddon. Like the house it was developed over the years and the influence of a number of historical periods and characteristics may be seen. The north aisle and chancel was added in the fourteenth century and the chancel early in the fifteenth.

Street scene at Sheldon. A former lord of the manor and principal landowner was the Duke of Devonshire. The population in the early 1930s was 100, at which time the workforce was mainly made up of farmers.

Sheldon's Church of St Michael and All Angels, erected in 1865, is a building of stone in the Gothic style, partially constructed with materials taken from an ancient edifice formerly standing in the village street. It consists of apsidal chancel, nave, south porch and a turret containing one bell. There were 140 sittings. The register of baptisms dates from 1813 and that of burials from 1853, other entries being made at Bakewell. There is a record of a singular marriage between a woman of eighty and a lad of fourteen at this chapel in the seventeenth century.

five

Edensor, Beeley
and Chatsworth

Above: The church of St Anne at Beeley is a building of stone consisting of chancel, nave, south porch and an embattled western tower. Its earliest portion is a round-headed Norman doorway and may date from 1150-'60. The north aisle, removed in 1819, was formerly separated from the nave by a Norman arcade with pointed arches. About a century later, during the Early English period, the chapel, then existing, was extensively rebuilt, and the present structure appears to belong to this style. The chancel and tower arches, as well as some features of the chancel and belfry windows, are Decorated. A window in the chancel and the battlements and pinnacles of the tower are Perpendicular. In 1819 the inhabitants applied to quarter sessions and obtained a brief for the repair of the fabric, and two other briefs were obtained for the same purpose in 1823 and 1826. Between 1182-'84 the church was thoroughly restored at a cost of £2,500. The register dates from 1538.

Below: Beeley post office containing refreshment rooms may be seen on the left, *c.* 1920. Post offices often feaured in Scrivens' picyures, maybe because they sold his cards.

Above: Beeley Church and vicarage, *c.* 1920.

Below: Chatsworth House from a print dated 1775. Originally, there was a Tudor building at Chatsworth built by Bess of Hardwick from 1552. The present Chatsworth house dates from 1686 to 1707 and is largely the work of the fourth Earl who, in 1694, became the first Duke of Devonshire. The 1,000-acre park was constructed by Capability Brown in 1761 for the fourth Duke, Lancelot (Capability) Brown. The sixth Duke caused the present 100-acre gardens to be laid out by Sir Joseph Paxton.

Chatsworth House is often described as the 'Palace of the Peak' or the true 'National Gallery of the North' as it houses not only one of Britain's but Europe's finest collections of art treasures on view in more than thirty rooms. These include the first Duke's painted hall and state apartments, the dining room and sculpture gallery and the nineteenth-century library.

Chatsworth House, Edensor Lodges.

Chatsworth House, for many years the ancestral home of the Dukes of Devonshire, is set in the heart of the Peak District National Park. Some unusual statistics include: The House has 1.3 acres of roof, under which there are 175 rooms, 3,426 feet of passages, 17 staircases and 359 doors, all lit by 2,084 light bulbs. There are 397 external window frames, 62 internal window frames, 5 roof lanterns and 60 roof lights with a grand total of 7,873 panes of glass. There are 27 baths, 55 wash hand basins, 29 sinks, 6 wash ups and 56 lavatories. Additionally, the Chatsworth Estate covers an area of 35,000 acres (14,000 hectares or 55 sq. miles) spread over more than 20 miles of Derbyshire and Staffordshire.

In the Gardens, Chatsworth. The 1,000-acre park that surrounds Chatsworth is open throughout the year at no charge. (2003)

The Gardens, Chatsworth House. In 2003 Chatsworth will celebrate the bicentenary of Joseph Paxton, one of the most dynamic figures of the nineteenth century and head gardener at Chatsworth for more than thirty years. He created the giant rock garden, the Emperor fountain and famous glasshouses.

In the Gardens, Chatsworth, *c.* 1920.

Entrance Lodge, Kitchen Garden, Chatsworth, *c.* 1920.

Queen Mary's Bower, Chatsworth, *c.* 1920.

Above: The South Front of Chatsworth House from the Lake. The house contains splendid displays of paintings, including work by Rembrandt, Van Dyck, Gainsborough and Freud, furniture, silver, tapestries and porcelain and a gallery of neo-classical sculptures. Famous curiosities include four royal thrones, a giant ancient Greek marble foot, a lace cravat carved from wood, the fan of a Rolls Royce jet engine and the unique illusionistic painting of a violin hanging on a door.

Right: The Tower, Chatsworth.

The French Garden, Chatsworth House, *c.* 1920.

The Tree Fountain, Chatsworth House. The 105-acre garden at Chatsworth is beautiful in all seasons. As well as the maze, rose, cottage and kitchen gardens, there are five miles of walks with rare trees, shrubs, fountains and ponds. Water pours down the steps of the first Duke's cascade and shoots from the branches of the willow tree fountain ('the squirting tree').

The French Garden, Chatsworth, *c.* 1920.

Sir Joseph Paxton's Greenhouse, Chatsworth, *c.* 1920.

Above: The design of the brick-built Chatsworth Institute, Edensor, dating from around 1775, has been attributed to James Paine, though the large porch may have been added at a later stage.

Right: Post office and St Peter's Church, Edensor, the latter being completed to the designs of Sir George Gilbert Scott in 1867. The church incorporates some old fabric.

The vast monument to William, the First Earl of Devonshire (1616) and Henry Cavendish (1625), housed in the chapel at the east end of Edensor Church. The two bodies have been placed under a low four-poster with black columns and a black covering slab. Henry is seen as a skeleton on a straw mat, William in his shroud with face exposed.

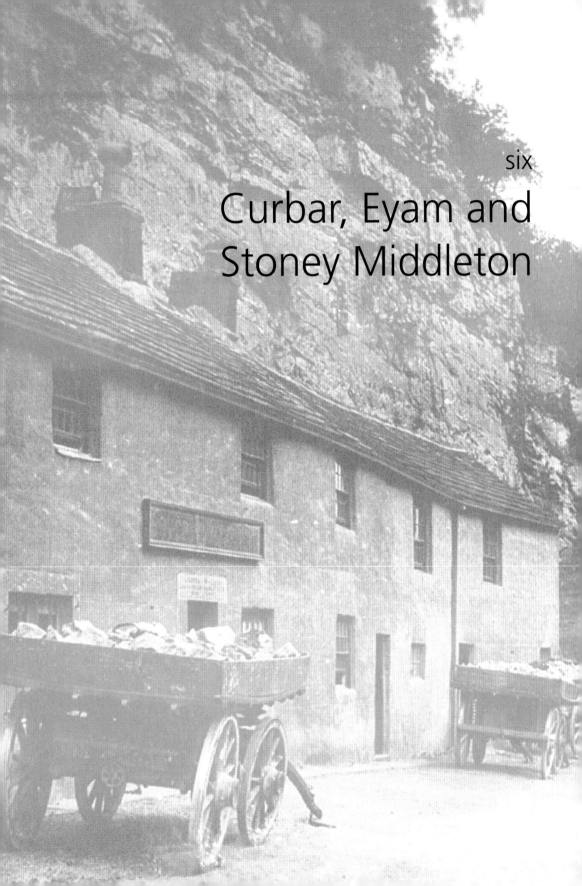

six

Curbar, Eyam and Stoney Middleton

Broom Close Farm, Curbar, *c.* 1930. The added bay windows arguably spoil the building's appearance.

Green Farm, Curbar, *c.* 1912.

An interesting feature of Curbar is the Old Round House, a village lock up with a curious conical roof.

Chatsworth View, Curbar, *c.* 1912.

Above: Anniversary service in the Cucklet Dell, Eyam, on 28 August 1910, for those who died in the Plague. The village was almost depopulated by the terrible visitation of the Plague in 1666. The disease, it is said, was brought from London to Eyam in a box of clothes sent to a tailor who resided near the Church. Five sixths of the inhabitants were carried off in sixteen months. The church and churchyard were closed and the dead buried in graves hastily in the gardens and fields. Divine service was performed, during this period, by the rector William Mompesson (who was later to die himself) in a dell a short distance from the village, bounded on one side by craggy rocks and overhung by trees on the other, where he preached from a lofty perforated rock, since called 'Cucklet Church'. A commemoration service is held there annually on the last Sunday in August. During the continuance of the plague a line was drawn round the village, the neighbouring inhabitants bringing supplies of food and leaving them upon certain stones, afterwards returning for the value, which was deposited in a trough of spring water for purification.

Opposite above: Club cottages, Curbar. The Great Plague hit Curbar early in the seventeenth century, some thirty years earlier than Eyam. Curbar has a Church, All Saints (1868), by architect Salvin Jun.

Opposite below: Trough and well, Curbar, with Froggat Edge, a gritstone escarpment on the eastern side of the village. The trough here is circular and the well is covered. Curbar is five miles north-west of Bakewell and is described as a hillside village, being popular with both climbers and walkers.

Above: Eyam village is often described as one of the most romantic and interesting in the Peak. It is built on a series of caverns, some of which have been explored to a great extent, chiefly for the beautiful stalactite with which they abound. The scenery around is highly varied and picturesque. Northward is a mountain range nearly 400 feet in height above the level of the village, which itself is 800ft above sea level, and which perfectly shelters the village from the northern winds.

Right: The Rectory, Eyam, was built around 1768 for the Revd Thomas Seward but has since been demolished. Parts of it however, including the staircase and Mompesson study have been incorporated in a modern building.

Eyam village. Early industries included lead mining and silk weaving. Later one of the chief industries of the place was the manufacture of boots, shoes and ankle straps.

Eyam, where the population at the outset of the twentieth century was 946.

Eyam with the church in the distance. Miss Anna Seward, poet and daughter of the Revd Thomas Seward, sometime rector of Eyam, was born there in 1747, and died at Lichfield on 25 March 1809. Peter Cunningham, the poet, was curate at Eyam for a while, but afterwards went to Chertsey, Surrey, where he died in July 1805.

The church of St Lawrence (formerly known as St Helen from the edifice having a chapel of that name) is an impressive stone edifice, consisting of chancel, clerestoried nave of four bays, aisles, south porch and an embattled western tower with crocket pinnacles. The chancel and the tower were rebuilt about 1615; the church was restored in 1868 and the south aisle in 1882. The register dates from 1630. In an area of the church, a small exhibition gives details about the Plague saga.

Above: Eyam village. This is probably one of the best-preserved villages because of its many impressive old houses. Eyam Moor lies above the village. Interestingly, Eyam once had one of the earliest public water supplies (from 1558) of anywhere in the vicinity, traces of which still remain.

Left: Mr White's Tea Rooms, Eyam. Curiously the village only has one pub – the Miner's Arms, dating from 1630, which is supposed to be one of Derbyshires' most haunted buildings.

Plague Cottages, Eyam. A number of cottages in the village display plaques giving historical details and the part their earlier inhabitants played in the Plague epidemic. The village endured the Plague for eighteen months, ending in October 1666. In that time it had claimed about a third of the inhabitants (260 out of a total of 800).

The Old Hall, in the main street at Eyam. The premises were completed in 1676 (a date noted on a rainwater-head). It is a three-storey house, the front being half the shape of the letter 'H'. The east front has three gables and the windows have hood-moulds. The house's central gateway extends onto the street. The property is the exclusive home of the Wright family who opened their house to the public in 1992. The property is open during the summer months to visitors and it retains the intimate atmosphere of a much-loved private home.

Street scene, Stoney Middleton, *c.* 1912.

Street scene, Stoney Middleton, where the old custom of well dressing takes place in late July.

Above: Street scene, Stoney Middleton,
c. 1912.

Left: The Avenue, Stoney Middleton,
c. 1910.

Above: Stoney Middleton from the Bank, *c.* 1910.

Right: Stoney Middleton's Church of St Martin, situated at the lower end of the village, is an octagonal building erected in 1759, in place of an earlier structure, consisting as far as is known, of a simple chancel and nave. The embattled western tower is a low structure in the Late Perpendicular style. This was built by Joan Eyre to commemorate her husband's safe return from Agincourt in 1415. A mural tablet of Derbyshire marble was placed in the nave in 1888 by members of the Clerical Greek Testament Meeting, as a memorial to the late Revd Urban Smith MA, incumbent of this parish between 1834-'88. The church was repaired in 1898 at a cost of £50, and in 1900 a new organ was erected at a cost of £200. The churchyard is very small, but a new cemetery was laid out a short distance away, and was consecrated by the Bishop of Lichfield on 11 October 1878. There were 250 sittings. The register dates from 1715 for all entries.

Above: The Lover's Leap Inn is under the rock Lover's Leap at Stoney Middleton. In *History of the Village of Stoney Middleton* (1910) by Thos. E. Cowen, transcribed by Rosemary Lockie (February 2003), it is stated: 'It was kept for many years by Mr Samuel Mason, who in conversation told many stories of bye-gone days. When all the lime-kilns were in full swing, day after day forty or fifty carters were to be seen waiting their turn to be supplied, as early as four and five o'clock in the morning. The carts came down from a wide district, Barlow, Brampton, Chesterfield, and Holymoorside being always represented. Many a battle royal was fought by the carters during their long wait. All this has changed, and the industry has disappeared with the exception of Mr. Henry Goddard's kiln'.

Below: An old corner of Stoney Middleton. In *A History of the Village of Stoney Middleton* it is stated: 'Stoney Middleton is a romantic village situated five miles from Bakewell, five from Tideswell, and twelve from Sheffield. A brook running through the village divides it from the neighbouring village of Eyam. Some of the houses are situated one above the other, on ledges of rock which seem to be almost inaccessible, and the others are scattered'.

Above: Lover's Leap, Stoney Middleton. Around 1760, the love-stricken Hannah Baddeley threw herself from the top of the perpendicular precipice seen here. Miraculously she sustained little injury. The brambles and rocky projections went some way to cushion her fall. After that horrifying experience she seemingly came to her senses and eventually died a spinster, but this was only two years later. The man who was the cause of her suicidal attempt was William Barnsley.

Below: Main Street, Stoney Middleton, *c.* 1910.

Shining rock and Eyam Dale, Stoney Middleton, *c.* 1912.

The Hall, Stoney Middleton, situated on the right of the road from Bakewell at the entrance to the village and a little to the east of the church, dating from Elizabethan or Jacobean times. Featuring two pointed gables, it was altered during the early nineteenth century. According to *A History of the Village of Stoney Middleton* (2003) 'In former times this residence, then much smaller, was a farmhouse, occupied by Squire Radford.'

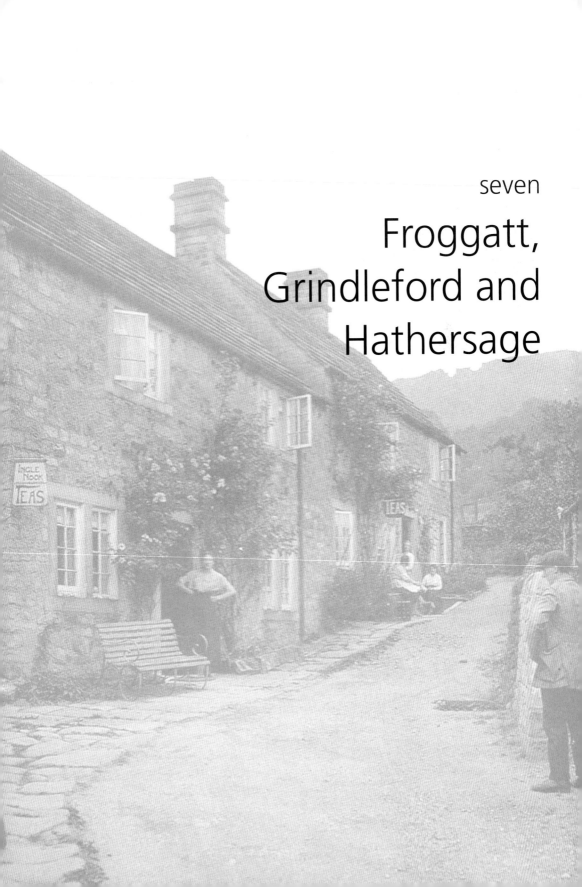

seven

Froggatt, Grindleford and Hathersage

Above: Froggatt village, on the east bank of the Derwent, lies six miles north-west of Bakewell and around three-and-a-half miles north of Chatsworth. The population at the time the picture was taken was around 154.

Left: Cottages and rocks, Froggatt, *c.* 1912.

Froggatt Edge, featuring the Chequeres Inn (centre) which was converted from a row of six cottages in around 1632. Other features of the village include an eighteenth-century bridge and a Wesleyan Reform chapel.

Froggatt Edge and village. Froggatt Edge is a steep ridge of grit stone rock, rising to a great height to the east. A Methodist chapel in the village was built in 1834.

Froggatt Edge from Stoke Hall, *c.* 1920.

New Froggatt Bridge from Froggatt Edge, *c.* 1920.

At the Crossroads, Froggatt, *c.* 1920.

View along Spooner Lane, Froggatt, *c.* 1920.

The Moorlands, Froggatt, *c.* 1912.

The small village of Grindleford, part of which can be seen here, is six miles north of Bakewell and is dissected by the River Derwent. It also lies adjacent to Padley Gorge.

The Lake, Lonshaw Lodge, Grindleford. North of Grindleford village is the Longshaw Estate, which once belonged to the Dukes of Rutland. The National Trust acquired the area, a superb expanse of moorland and woodland, in the 1970s. It currently boasts a visitor's centre which is open daily from June to September.

Street scene, Grindleford, *c.* 1920. The area has become a pleasant and desirable commuter village for those working in Sheffield and Chesterfield. Note the 'High Class Confectioner's' cart on the left.

Commercial Hotel, Grindleford, *c.* 1920.

Grindleford from Froggatt Edge, *c.* 1915.

Grindleford. The picture probably dates from the late 1920s.

A panoramic view of Grindleford. Grindleford actually comprises Grindleford itself, on the west bank of the Derwent, and Padley on the east bank.

Goat's Cliffe Cottages, Grindleford. This small village resides at an ancient crossing point of the River Derwent, and adjacent to the present stone road bridge is the old Toll House

Leam Hall, Grindleford from the lake, *c.* 1920.

Looking up Sir William Hill, Grindleford.

The Maynard Arms Hotel, Grindleford.

Above: Upper Padley, Grindleford. An interesting village feature of the village is the restored Padley Chapel (the original gatehouse). This is all that is left of the Fitzherbert's family home, Padley Hall, built around 1400. The family were devout Catholics and often sheltered priests at the Hall at a time when any priest seen administrating Roman rites was judged to be a traitor to his sovereign and country. Every year Roman Catholics make a pilgrimage to the chapel on the Sunday closest to 12 July in memory of two priests, Nicholas Garlick and Robert Ludlam, who were caught sheltering there and subsequently found guilty of high treason and condemned to death. These two eventually became known as the Padley Martyrs.

Longshaw Lodge, Grindleford, originally erected around 1827 as a shooting box for the Duke of Rutland.

Cottages in Eyam Road, Grindleford.

Commercial Row, Grindleford, *c.* 1920.

In Padley Woods, Grindleford, *c.* 1920.

Railway station and tunnel, Grindleford. Extending over three-and-a-half miles beneath Totley moor (from Totley in Sheffield to Grindleford) the Totley railway tunnel is a remarkable engineering feat. Work started in 1888 and despite many setbacks was completed around 1894.

Railway station, Grindleford.

Railway station and tunnel, *c*. 1925. The railway station notice on the left states: 'Grindleford for Baslow, Eyam and Stoney Middleton'.

The Church of St Helen's at Grindleford, comprising chancel, south chapel , vestries and temporary nave dates from 1909-'10. It was built to provide a place of worship for the population increase in Grindleford following the completion of the Totley railway tunnel in around 1994. E.A.J. Maynard, whose family had owned land in Nether Padley for generations, gave one-and-a-half acres of land for the site. The stone used in its construction came from the nearby Stoke quarry. Taking less than a year to complete (work began in November 1909) the dedication was undertaken by the Bishop of Southwell on 21 September 1910.

Grindleford incorporates Grindleford itself, situated on the west bank of the River Derwent, and Padley on the east side.

E.L.S.171-40. In Padley Woods, Grindleford.

Above: In Padley Woods, Grindleford.

Left: St Michael's Church at Hathersage has an impressive lofty position in the village, with superb views of the Derwent valley. Some work can be dated from 1381, but it is believed certain parts may hark back to the twelfth century. The interior contains some interesting monuments of the ancestors of the Earls of Newburg. At one time on the south side of the churchyard, a spot marked by two stones was pointed out as the place of interment of Little John (thought to have been a native of Hathersage but born at Loxley eight miles away), the favourite companion of Robin Hood. During 1784 a thigh bone measuring 30ins was exhumed from a grave about 11ft long, but it has since disappeared. The grave can be found on the southern boundary of the churchyard. The church has a Perpendicular west tower with diagonal buttresses. The interior contains an impressive collection of Eyre family brasses.

Hathersage is an attractive area situated in the Derwent valley, Derbyshire, and the Peak District National Park. The village/small town has several pubs and hotels, the sixteenth-century George Hotel and the Hathersage Inn, with the Little John Inn not far away.

For centuries Hathersage was a small agricultural village with cottage industries making brass buttons and wire. This changed in the mid-eighteenth century when a Henry Cocker opened the Atlas Works, and began manufacturing wire. Later other mills opened to make needles and pins. Umbrella frames were also produced. In the nineteenth century smoke from the five mills made Hathersage a dirty place to live. Wire and needle-making was transferred to Sheffield at the end of the nineteenth century and the last mill closed in 1902, though some are still extant today.

On its east side Hathersage is overlooked by moorland and a line of grit stone edges. Consequently, it is popular with walkers and rockclimbers alike. The village was formerly noted for a number of activities, which included the production of millstones and grit stone. Also, in 1845, Charlotte Brontë stayed at Hathersage Vicarage and is believed to have based some of her novel *Jane Eyre* on the area, and indeed the heroine's surname on a well-known local family.

North Lees Hall is an Elizabethan manor house and features as 'Thornfield Hall' in Charlotte Brontë's novel *Jane Eyre*, the character Mrs Rochester jumping from the roof to her death. North Lees was built by Robert Eyre of Highlow and was one of seven halls built by him for his seven sons. These premises with a tall square tower and a long adjoining wing, are rated as one of the finest Elizabethan buildings in the region.

Toad Mouth Rock, near Hathersage, *c.* 1920.

The Weir, Hathersage, *c.* 1920.

eight

Millers Dale and Tideswell

Above: The limestone dale, Miller's Dale, stretches along part of the River Wye from Chee Dale to Water cum Jolly Dale. Monsal Trail runs the length of the dale. Miller's Dale was once part of the Midland railway line linking Buxton to London.

Right: During the nineteenth century the village of Miller's Dale grew in size due to an influx of railway men and quarry workers.

Miller's Dale, where an abundance of fauna may be seen.

It is amazing that not far from the tranquility of scenes like the one depicted here stood the notorious Litton Mill. It had a bad reputation for the way it treated its workforce, which included paupers and orphaned children. Quite often they worked long hours and had to endure little food, cramped accommodation and beatings by the Needham family who owned the mill.

Bridge and Church, Miller's Dale. The Church of St Anne's, nestling on the hillside dates from 1879 and was probably designed by H. Cockbain.

Opposite, above: Tideswell's Church of St John the Baptist is known as the 'Cathedral church of the Peak'. It is one of the largest churches in the area and is a cruciform building of stone. The church replaced a smaller building of Norman origin and belongs almost exclusively to the Decorated style of the latter half of the fourteenth century. It has been little altered since this time and consists of an unusually large chancel, clerestoried nave, aisles, transepts, a south porch with parvise and a lofty embattled tower at the west end, with battlemented, turret-like pinnacles at the angles, terminating in crocket spirals. The church is thought to have been built with the profits of the medieval lead and wool trades. The stained east window was inserted in 1876 by Cecil G. Savile Foljambe esq. (afterwards Earl of Liverpool) in memory of his first wife Louise (Howard), (d.1871), and of the Foljambe family who were great benefactors of the church. Some restoration to the church occurred in 1875.

The chancel, Tideswell Church. In the centre of the chancel lies the altar tomb of Sir Samson Meverill, a local knight and landowner (1388-1462). It is believed that he may have fought at Agincourt.

Fountain Square, Tideswell. The area is one of the most ancient settlements in the Peak District, and is situated in a dale in the high limestone plateau of the White Peak. The name of Tideswell may have been derived from 'Tide's Well', Tide probably being the name of an Anglo-Saxon settler. Tideswell is recorded in the Domesday Book, and a charter for a market was granted in 1251. From medieval times to the nineteenth century the village was a centre for the lead-mining industry.

nine

Castleton and
Hope

The parish of Bamford is on the borders of Yorkshire, and is ten miles east from Chapel-en-le-Frith, twelve north from Bakewell, twelve west from Sheffield and 162 miles from London. During the mid-nineteenth century there was a large factory for doubling cotton, which gave employment for upwards of 800 hands. The population around that time was 857. During the first quarter of the twentieth century it had risen to just under 1,000.

Street scene at Bamford. *Kelly's Directory* of 1931 states that 'the village is lighted with gas and electricity, and supplied with water conveyed in pipes from springs on Bamford Edge, a mountain ridge over 1,600ft high, on the southern slopes of which the village lies.'

The Anglers Rest Hotel, Bamford. Noted landlords of the inn have included James Tagg and Rene Wm. Pradier.

Street scene at Bamford, *c.* 1915.

Aerial view of Castleton, nicknamed the 'Gem of the Peaks' perhaps because it has so many attractions, including the keep of Peveril Castle (Castleton is named after the castle), its four show caves, Winnets or Windgates-road, Mam Tor and the Speedwell, Odin, Trecliff and Water Hull mines.

Aerial view of Castleton, which lies between the Dark Peak (in the north) and the White Peak (in the south). The Dark Peak is noted for the grit stone edges and the south for its Limestone plateaus. One of the ancient ceremonies that still takes place in Castleton is Oak Apple Day. This occurs on 29 May and celebrates the end of winter, and the restoration of Charles II to the throne in 1660 after the rule by Oliver and Richard Cromwell (1653–'58 and 1658–'59).

Castleton Church, dedicated to St Edmund is of small dimensions, and though modernised and much altered still retains some vestiges of the early English, its original style. It has a fine Norman arch across the nave, which was constructed from 1190 to 1250. The tower was added between 1450-1500 and more additions were made in the nineteenth century.

Castleton from the Castle showing Lose Hill, *c.* 1920.

Castleton from Goose Hill, showing Mam Tor, a grand mountain composed of grit stone and shale, rising majestically above the village. Due to the nature of this rock, its surface is subject to constant disintegration by the action of the atmosphere, and the loosened fragments fall and accumulate at its foot. From this circumstance it is also called the Shivering Mountain.

Mam Tor, Castleton, is composed of horizontal layers of shales and grit stone and is one of the highest summits of the Peak District. It reaches a height of 1,300ft and has on its summit the remains of a double-ditched camp of sixteen acres and two barrows. At its base is the famous Odin lead mine, and in various places fluorspar, bitumen and manganese were obtained.

Above: Mam Tor, composed of horizontal layers of shales and grit stone, Castleton. From the top panoramic views of the Hope Valley may be seen.

Right: Peak Cavern Gorge and Peveril Castle. Castleton boasts four show caves comprising the Blue John Cavern, Treak Cliff Cavern, Speedwell Cavern (all grouped around the Winnets pass) and the great Peak Cavern. This cave was formally known as the 'Devils Arse' before being called Peak Cavern, however has recently been renamed the 'Devils Arse'. It is below Peveril Castle in the centre of the village, having the largest natural cave entrance in Britain and the second largest in the world. Beyond the entrance a narrow passage leads to a chamber called the Bell-House.

Village scene showing tea rooms, Castleton, *c.* 1920. This view might not have been taken by Scrivens as another photographer's inscription can be seen on the card. But Scrivens had a habit of 'buying' views and then putting his initials on them.

Street scene, Castleton. The village is clustered around a central square.

The Bargates, Castleton, *c.* 1920.

Entrance to Blue John Cavern, Castleton. Today the cavern is world famous, being home to eight of the fourteen known varieties of Blue John Stone – a beautiful and ornamental fluoro-spar. The mineral has been mined here for centuries and continues to be so in the winter months.

Entrance to Blue John Cavern. The traditional methods of turning Blue John are currently still being used, and the skills of craftsmen working in the original Blue John craft shop in the village of Castleton enables the visitor to view this unique stone at its best.

Entrance to Speedwell Cavern. This is near the foot of the Winnets road and is reached by a descent of 100 steps, at the bottom of which is a great level covered with water. This is crossed by boat, and the cavern is entered. It is believed to be 600ft high, and to be bounded by a gulf several hundred feet deep, into which the water rushes with appalling noise.

Cross Street, Castleton, *c.* 1920, with the Bull Head Inn near the centre of the picture.

Cross Street, Castleton.

Main Street, Castleton, with the Castle Hotel at the centre of the picture.

The Old Hall, Castleton, c. 1925.

Peak Cavern, also called the Devil's Cave, Castleton, is at the end of the remarkable glen or hollow in which the village stands. It consists of a series of vast chambers and passages in the interior of the rock on which the castle is built. The entrance is a great dark arch, 120ft wide and 40ft high. One of the chambers is 200ft square and 120ft high. A broad stream separates the cavities, and is crossed by a ferry. The entire length of the cavern is said to be 2,250ft. Various names are given to the chambers, one being called the Bell House, another the Chancel, others include the Devil's Cellar and Halfway House.

The Square and Peveril Castle, Castleton. The village is mainly centred round this square.

The Bridge, Castleton, *c.* 1920, with tea rooms to the right.

The Sicket, Castleton.

The Winnets, or Windgates-road, Castleton, is a very steep descent, a mile long, forming the approach to Castleton from Chapel-en-le-Frith and winding, in some parts between precipices 800ft high. The road is so called on account of the rush of wind constantly sweeping through it.

Wesleyan chapel, Castleton.

Ruins of the Keep, Peveril Castle. William Peveril, thought to have been an illegitimate son of William the conqueror, built this Norman castle after the Norman conquest of 1066 to oversee the King's Royal Forest of the Peak. In fact Peveril was granted the title of Bailiff of the Royal Manors of the Peak. The Keep which survives today dates from 1175, and was built under the auspices of Henry II. Earlier, in 1157, Henry had accepted there the submission of King Malcolm of Scotland. For a time the castle was held by King John, but was captured and retained for some years by the barons. Edward III granted it to his son, John of Gaunt, who was afterwards entitled Duke of Lancaster and the castle became what it still remains, part of the duchy of Lancaster. It was a fortress of considerable size and strength, having walls between 8 and 9ft thick and 20ft high. The ruins consist of the donjon, or Keep; a massive tower, 55ft high, standing on the edge of the rock; and part of the gateway on the north side. It is said that a tournament was held here by William Peveril. The rock on which the castle stands is a mass of limestone, the prevailing rock in the district. The castle fell into decline after Tudor times, and by the seventeenth century only the keep was utilised – as a courthouse. When this ceased the castle gradually fell into ruins. English Heritage now cares for the castle which is open to the public throughout the year.

St Peter's Church and War Memorial at Hope. The church, standing on a slight elevation by the roadside near the River Peveril, is a building of stone, consisting of chancel, clerestoried nave of four bays, aisles, south porch and a western tower with an Early-English broach spire. The chief characteristics of the exterior are Perpendicular, the outer walls of the clerestory, transepts and choir being surmounted by embattled parapets, with occasional crocket pinnacles. The whole church, excepting the tower and spire, was perhaps rebuilt about the beginning of the fourteenth century. The church plate is dated 1711. The chancel was restored in 1881 at a cost of £1,195, and the church completely restored in 1887 at a cost of £2,050, defrayed by Edward Firth of Birchfield. The War Memorial is of local stone, and at this time was inscribed with the names of the men from the parish who gave their lives in the First World War, 1914-18.

The Guest House, Hope, *c.* 1920.

Hope was formerly a market town under the Fitzwarrens, who had a castle here. In a extract from the *National Gazetteer* in 1868, the following curious information is revealed: '[Hope] is situated on the river Noe, and contains Bradwell, Brough, Fairfield, and fifteen other townships... The bodies of two people buried in the moors in 1674 were found twenty years after in an preserved state, the skin being soft, and resembling tanned leather. Joseph Hall esq., is lord of the manor. A market for cattle is held on the last Wednesday in every month... The inhabitants are engaged in the cotton, rope, hat and lace manufactures. The larger part of the land is in moorland'.

Left, above: Edale Road, Hope, *c.* 1920.

Left: Old Hall Hotel, Town End, Hope.

Below: Town End, Hope, *c.* 1920.

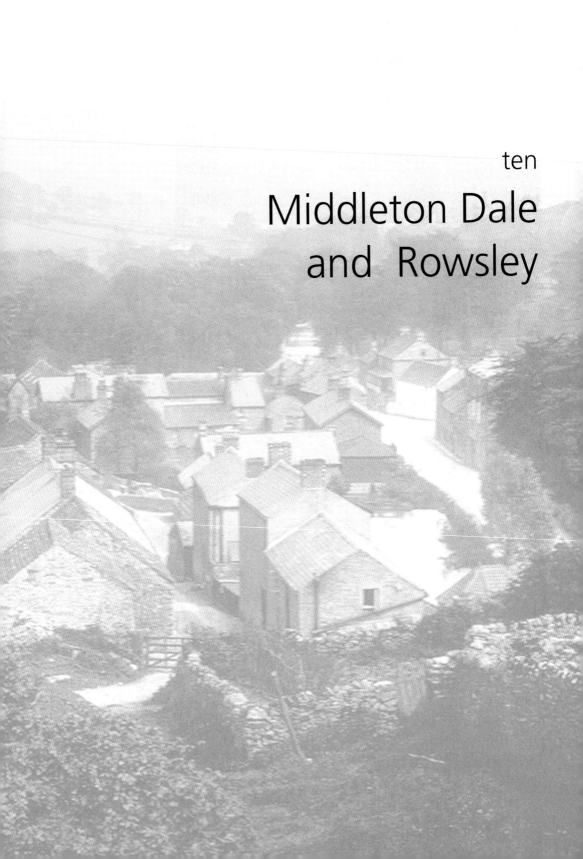

ten

Middleton Dale
and Rowsley

Shining Rock, Middleton Dale, *c.* 1930.

View of Middleton Dale, *c.* 1920.

View of Stoney Middleton village, which is at the foot of Middleton Dale. The area is noted for its rock climbs such as the one at Windover Buttress. In addition, there is also some interesting pot holes, one of the most noted being the Calswark Cavern.

A panoramic view of Rowsley.

Above: Rowlsey Bridge, *c.* 1920.

Below: Entrance to the Peacock Inn, Rowsley, *c.* 1920.

Below, Right: On the Wye, Rowsley, *c.* 1920.

Church Lane, Rowsley, *c*. 1915.

Peacock Inn, Rowsley, *c*. 1920.

Above: The River Wye at
Rowsley, *c.* 1918.

Right: View of Rowsley
Church, *c.* 1920.

Right below: Street scene,
Rowsley, *c.* 1920.